The Art of Tyranny I
Introduction to Truthful Media Content
Civilization 2.0, 3.0, and Beyond Series

First Edition
©Copyright 2023 All Rights Reserved
Author: Cornel Chavez, M.A. Publisher: Gebsmedia

Gebsmedia
gebsmedia.com

Gebsmedia

CONTENTS

Poster Title: The law-mills again at work (1900)   img1
By: Udo Keppler (American, 1872 – 1956)

Udo J. Keppler, known from 1894 as Joseph Keppler Jr., was an American political cartoonist, publisher, and Native American advocate. The above is a black and white version of his poster. The color version can be seen online (see notes at the end of this book).

The above poster depicts the United States capital building as a mill or factory that overproduces massive numbers of needless corrupt laws that are drowning Lady Justice. The overproduction of scores of needless, corrupt laws has been part of the art of tyranny imposed on humanity by malevolent ruling elites since the first written laws in human history were written down on clay tablets in ancient Kiengir (Sumer) long before the Code of Hammurabi was created in ancient Babylon. Babylon got its cuneiform writing system, its mathematics, and much of its way of life from Kiengir.

Introduction

This is the third book in our series, "Civilization 2.0, 3.0, and Beyond Series" which is a book series that establishes that we are very far from being an advanced civilization and that we should explore ideas that will accelerate the advancement of humanity towards a higher level of societal organization that can provide greater levels of safety and security for sovereign individuals.

This book series also emphasizes the need for a formal "Civilization Science" that will guide humanity's progress towards a much brighter future that provides a greater level of safety and security for individuals against the endless wars, horrible levels of crime rates across the globe including war crimes, predatory ideologies, financial uncertainty experienced by billions of people worldwide, out-of-control, malicious and corrupt shepherd ruling elites, deadly diseases, democide, predatory taxation, and other serious problems that currently plague humanity.

This volume introduces the topic of the art of tyranny and the process of truthful media content. To understand the need for truthful media content, we first look at the indoctrinating, propaganda narratives of shepherd ruling elites.

Chapter One

The Media Oligarchy Versus a Decentralized Media

"We should not, like sheep, follow the herd of creatures in front of us, making our way where others go, not where we ought to go." --Seneca

Fortunately for humanity, malevolent, predatory shepherd ruling elites have not yet developed a complex, scientifically-based, totalitarian governance system that is driven by artificial intelligence (AI) to rule over what they view as vast human herds of exploitable people. Their tyrannical rule is still a sinister work of art that can be brutal oppression inflicted on humanity by the weaponization of governance systems against the people, false religious narratives that empower tyrannical ruling elites, countless numbers of burdensome, needless written laws no one person can count in a lifetime, and malevolent, groupthink indoctrinating propaganda narratives. Unfortunately for humanity, the time is fast approaching when narcissistic, psychopathic, Machiavellian ruling elites will have the technology to control every minute of a sovereign individual's life if such tyrants are not stopped by a social force of freedom-loving individuals. Humanity needs to develop a "Civilization Science" that will help us develop a decentralized, self-governing, network-based governance system. Such a decentralized governance network (DGN) will greatly weaken the ability of malevolent ruling elites to gain enough power to forcibly implement an AI-driven, scientifically-guided totalitarian governance system to rule over what they view as vast exploitable human herds who are herded into oppressive social and psychological corrals.

One of the malevolent forms of control used in the past and today to control the billions of sovereign individuals in the world is the usage of malevolent indoctrinating propaganda narratives. Groupthink, indoctrinating narratives have been one of the most powerful methods of mind control used by predatory shepherd ruling elites to psychologically and socially control groups of people since Sumerian times over 5,000 years ago. From the image propaganda on the Sumerian Standard of Ur, King Culgi's (a.k.a. King Shulgi) written indoctrinating propaganda in ancient Kiengir and Josef Goebbels' Nazi, multi-media propaganda to today's "fake news," ruling elites continue to use groupthink, indoctrinating propaganda narratives to implement their psychological and social control over most of the human race. Since the bad side of human nature will never go away, malevolent, indoctrinating propaganda narratives will always be with us. Humanity needs to learn how to effectively counteract the malevolent indoctrinating propaganda narratives of predatory, shepherd ruling elites that have greatly helped them create and maintain the structure of a tyrannical Shepherd Social Hierarchy (SSH).

In a prior book, we introduced the Sumerian Indoctrination Principle (SIP) that recognizes that malevolent, indoctrinating propaganda narratives can be disguised as true knowledge acquisition in pedagogical systems as it was in ancient Kiengir and as it is today. The SIP also recognizes the deliberate, artful intertwining of indoctrination with entertainment media, political discourse, and all media. The SIP also acknowledges that malicious, indoctrinating propaganda narratives are created in the minds of malevolent individuals who are psychopathic and extremely narcissistic. Such Machiavellian personality types believe that they are shepherds of exploitable human herds, and since prehistoric times, the malevolence of shepherd ruling elites has manifested itself in many ways such as sending millions of men and boys to be butchered on slaughterhouse battlefields. Because of inbreeding, many predatory oligarchs such as the Pharoah Tutankhamun and the European Hapsburgs in the past were born with physical and mental disabilities that made them even more tyrannical. The malevolence of such predatory ruling elites point to the existence of a malevolent-shepherd archetype.

From King Culgi's own written description where he called himself the "herdsman" and "shepherd" of the Sumerian people, the Nazi propagandist in the 1900s who remarked that he could turn any nation into a "herd of pigs" if he could control the media, to the usage of the term, "herd immunity (referring to COVID-19)" used in the medical tyranny of this century, evil ruling elites have always believed that they have the right to forcibly tell others what to believe and how to live their lives. Shepherd ruling elites have always utilized many indoctrinating narratives to help them gather vast human herds into psychological and social corrals in the same way that animals are herded into and trapped in physical corrals built for all types of livestock. Malevolent, shepherd ruling elites throughout history have always exhibited a strong need to forcibly control the lives of sovereign individuals. Humanity must create and implement a network-based, self-governing media of the people, by the people, and for the people to counter the indoctrinating propaganda narratives of our current media oligarchy. Humanity needs to learn how the mindset of the malevolent-shepherd archetype artfully accomplished malicious control over the self-aware consciousness of billions of individuals throughout history so that humanity can develop defenses against the indoctrinating propaganda narratives launched against sovereign individuals.

Centralized Versus Network-Based Governance

Non-universally accepted belief systems, religions, and ways of life will always exist. Humanity needs a DGN that supports network protocols that allow peaceful co-existence between non-universal belief systems and non-universal theologies. A decentralized, network-based governance system should have as its highest priority the protection of the physical, social, psychological, and economic safety and security of the individual from oligarchs who try to universally impose only one way of life on all of humanity to the exclusion of other cultural options.

There have always existed in every part of the world oppressed people such as servants to the rich, slavery, starving children, and other exploited individuals in ancient Kiengir, Akkad, Babylon, Assyria, the Hittite Empire, ancient Persia, ancient Egypt, ancient Greece, ancient Rome, ancient China, ancient Japan, Medieval Europe, and every known human society. Why are there still such severely exploited people around the world today? Mankind has not been able to fully explain why a tyrant class, who are always a tiny percentage of any society, has always existed in every known human society since prehistoric times. Does our human biology naturally create only tyrannical SSHs or are we intelligent enough to design a more advanced civilization where our governance hierarchies are ruled by a Network of Sovereign Individuals (NSI)?

Ruling elites since Sumerian times have developed many malevolent, manipulative methodologies of human-herd gathering and control including pagan theologies, predatory written laws, predatory control over family relationships, predatory taxation, and other collectivist-based tactical and strategical authoritarian governance approaches to human-herd exploitation. Tyrannical shepherd ruling elites have always herded sovereign individuals onto groupthink pastures to feed on collectivist, indoctrinating propaganda narratives that have psychologically and socially corralled individuals to live in such a way that they are easily manipulated by a small group of tyrants who are always at the top of a SSH. Today, humanity's social hierarchy is still ruled by a tiny percentage of the world's population just as it was thousands of years ago in ancient Kiengir. Human history shows that humanity's social hierarchy has always been directly or indirectly ruled by malevolent, shepherd ruling elites. Can we stop living under a SSH and start to live in a Sovereign Individual Social Hierarchy (SISH)?

A DGN with large numbers of nodes of influence could greatly dilute the power of our current group of predatory, shepherd ruling elites. A self-governing, network-based media could also greatly weaken the current media oligarchy that continues to weaponize media against the freedoms of sovereign individuals.

The Media Oligarchy

In 1983, 50 corporations controlled most of the American media. Today, it is a much smaller group of corporations that control American media. According to one article, "...most of the media you consume is owned by one of six companies. These six media companies are known as The Big 6 ... the major outlets are almost all owned by these six conglomerates. To be clear, "media" in this context does not refer just to news outlets — it refers to any medium that controls the distribution of information. So here, "media" includes 24-hour news stations, newspapers, publishing houses, Internet utilities, and even video game developers." [1]

The centralization of media power described in the above quote means that only a handful of predatory, shepherd ruling elites, who are in reality a media oligarchy, have tremendous power to mentally herd large groups of sovereign individuals into any type of mental corral with groupthink, indoctrinating propaganda narratives that are launched with deadly precision through any type of media including videos, educational print media, advertisements to sell products or services, images, audio files, movies, posters, websites, radio, podcasts, and more. When a media oligarchy supports a murderous ruling elite class, the consequences can be deadly democide launched at sovereign individuals as was the case in Nazi Germany in the last century where millions of innocent men, women, and children were murdered by their NAZI govenment.

Asking ChatGPT the question, "Which dictators in the past committed democide?" returned the following answer: "Democide refers to the intentional killing of large numbers of people, usually by a government or its agents. Unfortunately, throughout history, there have been many examples of dictators who have committed democide. Here are a few examples:
Adolf Hitler: As the leader of Nazi Germany, Hitler oversaw the systematic genocide of six million Jews during the Holocaust, as well as the killing of millions of other people, including political dissidents, homosexuals, and Romani (a.k.a. Gypsies).

(quote continued)

Joseph Stalin: As the leader of the Soviet Union, Stalin was responsible for the deaths of millions of people through his policies of forced collectivization, the Gulag system of labor camps, and the Great Purge, which targeted political opponents and perceived threats to his regime.

Pol Pot: As the leader of the Khmer Rouge in Cambodia, Pol Pot oversaw a genocidal campaign in which an estimated 1.7 million people were killed or died as a result of forced labor, starvation, and disease.

Mao Zedong: As the leader of the Chinese Communist Party, Mao oversaw a number of campaigns that resulted in the deaths of millions of people, including the Great Leap Forward and the Cultural Revolution.

These are just a few examples, but unfortunately, there have been many other dictators throughout history who have committed democide."

With the invention of a complete writing system over 5,000 years ago, the first written groupthink, indoctrinating propaganda narratives began to appear as cuneiform writing on clay tablets, and those clay tablets have lasted for thousands of years as proof of the existence of the malevolent-shepherd archetype in ancient times. ChatGPT also answered the question, "Who invented the first complete writing system in human history?" with the following answer: "The Sumerians are credited with inventing the first complete writing system in human history, known as cuneiform. Cuneiform was developed in ancient Mesopotamia around 3400 BCE and was initially used to record economic transactions. Over time, cuneiform evolved into a full-fledged writing system that was used to record all kinds of information, including literature, laws, and religious texts.

Cuneiform was made up of a series of wedge-shaped marks that were pressed into clay tablets using a stylus. The marks represented words and concepts, and over time, the writing system became more complex, incorporating both logographic and phonetic elements.

Cuneiform was eventually replaced by other writing systems, such as the Phoenician alphabet and the Greek alphabet, but its impact on human history cannot be overstated. Without the invention of cuneiform, it is unlikely that we would have many of the historical records and literary works that have survived to this day."

In our first book in this book series, "Civilization Version 2.0 – Humanity's Future or Humanity's Extinction?" we established that we continue to live under a repressive SSH where a small group of tyrannical ruling elites utilize predatory shepherd-governance systems, weaponized indoctrinating propaganda narratives, and a media oligarchy to exploit what malevolent tyrants view as vast human herds of sheeple. We also established the need for humanity to create a DGN to dilute the tyrannical power of the current crop of predatory, shepherd ruling elites. The art of tyranny utilizes a potent methodology used by tyrants since ancient times which is the utilization of groupthink, indoctrinating propaganda narratives spread throughout human societies by a centralized media oligarchy within each country in the world. One way to combat this powerful foundational pillar of tyranny is to create a self-governing, network-based infrastructure that is focused on a decentralized media system that is of the people, by the people, and for the people. Such a decentralized, network-based media would constantly expose to the public the malevolent, indoctrinating propaganda narratives created by predatory, shepherd ruling elites.

The current Centralized Media Oligarchy (CMO) hides the truth with methodologies such as censorship, slyly distorted narratives, and outright lies. Human nature itself teaches us that the good side of human biological programming will always be with us, but it also shows us that the bad side of human biological programming will also be with us forever. It would not be productive to try to eradicate the powerful evil nature within the souls of the oligarchs who control the current CMO. You cannot eliminate evil, but you can protect yourself from evil tyranny. The best approach to neutralize the malicious, indoctrinating power of the current CMO is to create a decentralized media of the people, by the people, and for the people. A self-governing, network-based media could be a strong defense against being herded onto the ruling elite's groupthink pastures to feed on collectivist, indoctrinating propaganda narratives that have psychologically corralled individuals for thousands of years to live in such a way that has increased the wealth and sovereign political power of a cabal of tyrannical, shepherd ruling elites at the same time that the sovereignty of each individual is disempowered. A self-governing NSI should have more sovereignty than a small group of predatory, shepherd ruling elites. A NSI should be at the top of any governance hierarchy, not a malevolent cabal of shepherd ruling elites.

Chapter Two

Creating a Decentralized,
Self-Governing Media Network

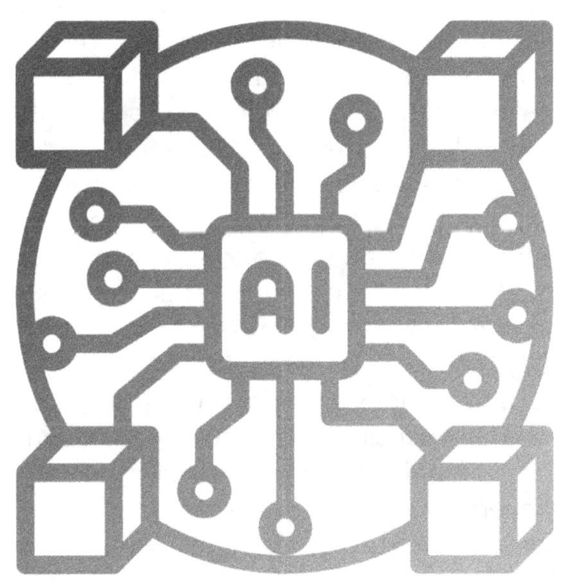

A Decentralized Self-governing Media Network (DSMN) that is of the people, by the people, and for the people constantly identifies and exposes the malicious strategies and tactics utilized by the CMO to collectively indoctrinate large groups of individuals. After identifying and exposing the media oligarchy's malevolent strategies and tactics, the DSMN should then formulate defensive solutions against such weaponized groupthink tyranny.

Essential to mentally dominating human herds is to hide liberating truth from those who are being exploited. Tyrannical shepherd ruling elites know that the "truth will set you free"[2] from the exploitation inflicted on you while you are forced to be trapped in your psychological and social corral. Hiding truth that empowers sovereign individuals is a potent weapon of psychological human herd control, and the CMO's current domination of the societal narratives allows them to hide liberating truth from a very large percentage of any country's population today.

There are many ways that are used in hiding the truth. One way is to outright lie or cunningly distort the reality of newsworthy events. For example, for a long time under the American Biden regime, the reality of the USA's southern border was hidden from the majority of Americans by the usage of false narratives. According to the Biden regime, the USA's southern border was safely under governmental control, but the reality is that it was far from being an international border where law and order prevailed. Under the Biden administration, the southern border was plagued with tons of deadly illegal drugs being brought across the border into the United States, horrible crimes against men, women, and children at the US southern border carried out by murderous criminal cartels, and millions of undocumented immigrants illegally entering into the USA causing social chaos on the southern border of the USA as well as inflicting a needless financial burden on American taxpayers.

Another way to hide the truth from sovereign individuals is censorship. Our current century has seen the rise of censorship to levels never seen before. From deplatforming on social media outlets to weaponizing the courts to silence anyone who speaks out against the CMO or the current crop of shepherd ruling elites.

Freedom of speech is a basic human right, but the current group of ruling elites in the CMO are constantly censoring any narrative that goes against their favored indoctrinating propaganda narratives. What are some of the ruling elite's favored narratives?

Unfortunately, the current crop of malevolent shepherd ruling elites in the USA favor indoctrinating propaganda narratives that support pedophilia, tyrannical Marxism, post-modernist thought, sexualizing young children, the breakup of natural family structures that support the well-being of every individual, the promotion of predatory taxation, burdening the people by imposing untold numbers of freedom-killing federal, state, and local laws on them that no one can completely count in a lifetime, and many of those sinister, totalitarian laws impose suffocating, needless control over the daily lives of individuals.

How can humanity greatly weaken the power of the tyrannical CMO? The good side of human nature will always be with us, but the bad side of human nature will also be with us forever. Building a decentralized, self-governing, network-based media of the people, by the people, and for the people where sovereign individuals could access truthful information about newsworthy events, entertainment options, social media options, and other media content would be more productive than trying to extinguish the evil in the minds of the media ruling elites. Evil never dies.

What would be the nature of such a DSMN? Transitioning from a society where societal narratives are dominated by a malevolent CMO to a society where a truthful DSMN dominates the societal narratives would be a monumental endeavor requiring enormous resources and a lot of hard work to create and maintain, but it is an essential structural building block in the construction of a more advanced human civilization that provides higher levels of safety and security for sovereign individuals against the artfully created tyranny of malicious, narcissistic shepherd ruling elites. One important function of a decentralized DSMN would be to build an online network infrastructure where all members of a DSMN could safely have access to and participate in the creation of analyses of all the media content generated by the CMO which would be a strong counterweight against the CMO's indoctrinating propaganda narratives.

In the rest of this chapter is a generalized, simple overview of the characteristics and possible self-governance network architecture of any DSMN. An actual operational DSMN would be technologically, socially, financially, and psychologically a highly complex, constantly adapting entity whose in-depth description is well beyond the scope of this book.

The Fundamentals of a DSMN

Membership in a DSMN – To avoid the autocratic centralization of the DSMN that we now see with the domain name registrar system on the Internet, there should exist a number of decentralized DSMN registrars where producers of media content and consumers of media content can register their membership. Comparing a centralized domain name system with a decentralized domain name system illustrates the advantages of decentralizing network systems such as governance systems for freedom-loving individuals. The registration of domain names is overseen by the centralized Internet Corporation for Assigned Names and Numbers (ICANN). Owners of ICANN-based domain names are required to pay a yearly domain name registration fee, and their domain name can be shut down by indoctrination-loving governance systems at any time. In the decentralized blockchain/web3 domain name world, there are no recurring yearly renewal fees and domains are minted on the blockchain with zero gas fees. Web3 domain names have many more uses than the domain names under the ICANN governance system. When you build and verify your digital identity with your Web3 domain name you can log in seamlessly to applications, games and metaverses, make payments easier by simplifying lengthy crypto wallet addresses, and create and host websites that you fully own. The UnstoppableDomains.com website has more information about Web3 domain names. Malevolent governance systems would not be able to shut down your Web3 domain name website that is part of the decentralized Internet. A decentralized Internet would be a powerful part of any DSMN. Web3 domains are returning the power of the Internet to the people.

There are many advantages to decentralization in the realm of domain name ownership and also, many important advantages to **decentralizing humanity's media**. DSMN registrars could provide a searchable database for all types of media that is outside of the control of the CMO. Anyone looking for specific entertainment media, newsworthy event media, knowledge acquisition (pedagogical) media, or any other type of media outside of the tyrannical control of the CMO could easily search the information stored by such registrars that help them interact with the processes that reveal Truthful Media Content (TMC) as defined in Chapter Three of this book.

Membership in a DSMN includes media consumers who could review/critique any media they consume and participate in appropriate governance activities.

Self-Governance: The Founding Fathers of the USA believed in a representative governance system. An American DSMN should also have a representative governance system defined by a more advanced type of geofencing of large numbers of geographical nodes of influence within the physical boundaries of the USA. A more advanced type of governance geofencing should be developed. Each geographical node of societal influence should elect a sizeable number of representatives to oversee the creation and implementation of the DSMN's network protocols such as the criteria for the inclusion or exclusion of members, prohibiting the weaponization of media for malicious political purposes, selecting the type of network technology used by the DSMN, and how to monetize the efforts of the members of the DSMN. Right now, the malevolent CMO is supported by billions of dollars of advertising money, and those same advertising dollars should eventually be directed into the DSMN as more and more sovereign individuals search within the DSMN for media that is outside of the control the CMO or any malevolent, shepherd governance system.

Access to Newsworthy Events – Members and representatives of the DSMN should have the same access to newsworthy events as anyone working for the tyrannical CMO. An example is the White House press corps. Events such as White House news briefings should be virtual events so that all members and representatives of both the DSMN and the current CMO have the same access to the White House news briefings. Questions for the White House by both the DSMN and CMO could be queued so that some are answered during the White House news briefing and others are answered later by posting the answers online. In any case, members of both the DSMN and CMO should have equal access to any and all newsworthy events.

 Network Technology – The network technology needed by a fully functional DSMN should be highly secure. It should safely and securely tally votes by members so that any voting results are quickly available for decision-making purposes. It would need to provide the latest in virtual group event technology. All activities such as group meetings, meetings between representatives of the DSMN, and other activities should be recorded and kept in specific databases for access by all members at any time after such events.

The DSMN should also leave the client-server model and adopt a model such as the latest version of the SAFE Protocol [3] to ensure more protection from encroachment by malevolent governance systems or any of the bad actors in cyberspace. Nodes and clients that follow the SAFE Protocol model would have a much higher level of privacy and security. Such a decentralized model would make it impossible for the DSMN to be shut down by any external, malevolent governance system, hackers, or the CMO.

The accumulated information in the DSMN's databases should also be part of an Decentralized Knowledge Acquisition and Storage System (DKASS) which would help in evaluating any knowledge acquisition (pedagogical) media.

Linguistic Freedom - All languages change over time. Natural changes in language are fine, but when malicious, shepherd ruling elites attempt to forcibly change language for malevolent political reasons, language changes become weapons of tyranny. Forcing others to use desired political language through the use of weaponized laws, weaponized institutional policies and rules, or the usage of weaponized indoctrinating propaganda narratives should be strongly opposed by freedom-loving individuals. A DSMN should always carefully monitor and expose forced speech attempts so that all media consumers can be made aware and continually informed of such linguistic tyranny. Current forced speech examples include the forced use of certain pronouns to show submissive obedience to certain gender ideologies and the forced elimination of certain words that include certain spellings. For example, there has been a social push to eliminate using words that contain the letters "m-a-n" and "m-e-n." Instead of saying fire<u>man</u> or fire<u>men</u>, you are pressured to say firefighter or firefighters. The problem with such linguistic tyranny attempts is that there are many words and phrases in the English language that use these letters such as hu<u>man</u>, hu<u>man</u> race, police<u>men</u>, hu<u>man</u>ity, <u>man</u>kind and hu<u>man</u>kind.

Responsibilities of the Media Consumer - Teaching responsibility is always an important part of any civilization. A DSMN should always encourage media consumers to take the responsibility to always keep up with the latest technology that helps them in the process of TMC. You can provide many lessons and tools to help individuals uncover the TMC in any and all media, but it is the responsibility of each individual to avail themselves of such resources.

Artificial Intelligence (AI) - There will always be good AI and AI that mirrors the bad side of human nature of the people that create sinister AI. A DSMN should always monitor with SAI the AI used by its network technology, AI used to create content, AI used to allow or deny access to a DSMN, and AI used to distribute/deliver the content of information to media consumers within its network.

The creation and maintenance of a DSMN will always be a monumental, difficult task, but the alternative is to allow the CMO to propagate its corrupt, harmful, indoctrinating propaganda narratives without any constraints to its implementation of the SIP.

Patriotism - An American DSMN should support the positive characteristics of American patriotism. In the American experience, the good side of patriotism has been shown to unite people of different races and ethnic groups, different religions, and different belief systems to take actions that support the important ideas embodied in the US Constitution, the Bill of Rights, and other ideas that are part of a unique Americanism that is in opposition to Marxism and other insidious, collectivist, human-herd gathering ideologies.

Monetizing a DSMN - There are many ways to monetize a DSMN. The SAFE Network's (safenetwork.tech) utilization of a proxy coin (MaidSafeCoin) while building the decentralized network that can be later exchanged for Safecoin when the network is live is one idea. Individual media creators also have many ways to monetize their online presence. Attracting advertising dollars is a very important part of monetizing a DSMN. The highly censored media creators at infowars.com currently sell a proprietary line of health products to fund their operations. They also accept donations. Such online sites could also promote affiliate programs. Monetizing a DSMN is an essential part of its continued existence and there are a number of ways to monetize such a decentralized network.

The creation of a DSMN is a gargantuan task which would require an enormous amount of resources, but the cost of not creating such a DSMN of the people, by the people, and for the people would always leave humanity under the totalitarian control of a CMO.

Note: Mentioning websites, organizations, products, services, or businesses in this book is for informational purposes only to illustrate some of the ideas in this publication and does not constitute endorsement or support for any of these websites, organizations, products, or services cited in this book.

Chapter Three
Truthful Media Content

The First Amendment uses the word, "press," in its text. In today's world, the word "press" would more appropriately be referred to as the "media" or "media world" which includes all of the different forms of media outlets such as podcasts, websites, news outlets, social media, and others. Also, the First Amendment shown below speaks separately about the freedom of speech and the freedom of the press. Why it speaks of both of them separately is debatable.

The First Amendment: "Congress shall make no law respecting an establishment of religion, or prohibiting the free exercise thereof; or abridging the freedom of speech, or of the press; or the right of the people peaceably to assemble, and to petition the Government for a redress of grievances."

What were the stated and implied intentions of the Founding Fathers when they spoke separately about freedom of speech and freedom of the press? What exactly is the stated and implied meaning of the idea of the freedom of the press? Question One: Are outright lies by the American press protected by the First Amendment? Question Two: Are manipulative, indoctrinating propaganda narratives by the American press that are used to cover up the truth protected by the First Amendment? Logic would reveal that the Founding Fathers included the need for the freedom of an American press in the First Amendment because they wanted an American press to have the power to voice the true feelings of the American people against government tyranny, but when the answer to both questions one and two above is the word, "no," it also reveals that not all speech created by a malevolent press or media should be legally protected under the First Amendment's freedom of the press. Malevolent, indoctrination narratives represent the exercise of free speech, but not freedom of the press. Outright lies and malicious, defaming and/or indoctrinating narratives should never receive legal protection from lawsuits against such behavior.

Today, the CMO voices the opinions and feelings of a small group of predatory, shepherd ruling elites, and those elitist belief systems do not mirror the true belief systems of the majority of the sovereign American people. The freedom of the press was listed in the First Amendment along with other individual rights such as the freedom of religion because the Founding Fathers wanted Americans to be empowered to protect themselves against deceitful, artfully-created government tyranny.

Today, the press promotes many things that go against the will of the majority of the American people including the promotion in the American press of pedophilia, the sexual grooming of young children, censorship, predatory taxation, the weaponization of the courts against those who exercise free speech, the promotion of anti-religious laws, and the breaking up of innate family structures that naturally promote the health and happiness of individuals. The need for the formation of a DSMN that aggressively supports and protects the First Amendment is urgently needed to combat the malevolent indoctrination of the CMO. During the COVID-19 pandemic, the CMO supported shutting down churches, censorship of any information that went against the government's medical tyranny, and supported many government actions that went against the "right of the people peaceably to assemble."

Currently, the CMO continues its outright lies about anything it opposes, promotes anti-religious indoctrination, and other indoctrinating narratives that go against the belief systems of the majority of Americans and against the stated and implied ideas enshrined in the First Amendment. The implicature within the First Amendment is debatable, but after careful thought, the Founding Fathers' referral to a "press" was a referral to a truth-telling "press" that could freely launch truthful media content against malevolent government tyranny. Physical tyranny is easily understood when openly visible, but deceitful, skillfully-crafted, indoctrinating propaganda narratives can artfully and slyly enter into the minds of children and adults like a venomous, stealthy serpent that silently enters your house to put you in mortal danger. Ruling elite indoctrination puts your individual sovereignty in mortal danger when it controls your mind. A truthful press should be a weapon against stealthy indoctrinating propaganda narratives launched against the people.

What is truth and reality in media content? What is reality? What is truth? You could fill thousands of pages with text trying to define the dimensions of reality or truth. With regards to a functioning DSMN, what is more appropriate is the question, "What is truthful media content?" The essential purpose of a DSMN is to promote the creation of and access to truthful media content by everyone. To avoid long scholarly explanations of what is truth and what is reality, the term "Truthful Media Content (TMC)" should be thought of as an operational social and psychological process rather than a theory defined within an academic discipline.

When looking at a video advertisement to sell a specific product, TMC is a cognitive process where a media consumer uncovers the real meaning and purpose of the text, utterances and visual imagery of such a video. At the end of the TMC process, the media consumer uncovers all of the real messages embedded in the video advertisement. Each embedded message may be implied or openly stated. Within such an advertisement video there may be a brief social scene involving a few actors, and that contrived social interaction may be analyzed in certain ways such as linguistic pragmatics where it could be shown to contain symbolism and implicature promoting an extreme indoctrinating propaganda narrative. Since the utterances that describe the factual characteristics of the product being promoted in a video advertisement may not be sinister indoctrination, the purpose of the utterances in a contrived social interaction shown in such a video advertisement may be to slyly implant indoctrinating propaganda within the minds of the media consumer. TMC is the process of reaching an appropriate level of understanding of any media content where a media consumer can make an informed decision about any particular type of media content. A DSMN can greatly enhance the ability of any media consumer to make informed decisions about any media content by providing access to media reviews/critiques, social media input, professional reviews, information about media creators, lessons on how to analyze media content, and other important information. A particular media consumer may want to know if certain media creators are avowed Marxists if that media consumer is a refugee from a totalitarian Marxist country where they experienced brutal oppression under a communist regime. A religious father may want to know if certain entertainment content contains anti-religious indoctrinating narratives before letting his child view certain entertainment media. TMC means that there is the highest level of transparency about any media content that is available for public use. TMC means that any DSMN that provides access to live opinion-oriented media requires that such live online venues openly state their beliefs or biases on their podcasts, streaming programs, or other live media, so media consumers can make an informed decision about consuming such media content. Having an informed understanding about any type of media content means that media consumers are empowered to keep their own original beliefs from being contaminated by insidious narratives.

TMC is a social process that involves not only the media creators who strive to provide TMC, but also the media consumers themselves who must engage in a process of not only constantly evaluating media content, but also learning how to recognize media content that can provide TMC that gives them thrilling entertainment, positive knowledge acquisition, or even positive intellectual or spiritual growth. The problem with malevolent, shepherd ruling elites since prehistoric times is that they continue to erroneously believe that they should decide what media content the people can and cannot see. Ideally, a DSMN would provide all the access to media content and tools any media consumer needs to determine if any media content is TMC and/or how much indoctrinating narratives any media content may contain. Within any DSMN, the people decide what media content they can and cannot see, not psychopathic ruling elites. The entire cognitive process from intelligent TMC creation to informed TMC consumer consumption is very complex, but it can be systematized and delivered routinely to the media consumer through a safe and secure DSMN that is connected within a decentralized cyberspace.

The media consumer needs to realize that a DSMN can also contain knowledge acquisition content that can be part of a larger DKASS which includes AI-directed pedagogical and human pedagogical methodologies. Humanity's current knowledge acquisition and storage systems are at best piecemeal systems for the average media consumer. Malevolent governance systems currently do not make their databases readily available to sovereign individuals. Since our current governance systems in the world are controlled by a handful of ruling elites, much of the knowledge databases in the world are controlled by a few ruling elites. Humanity needs to build an DKASS that is outside of the control of malevolent ruling elites. A Civilization Science that is under the authority of a decentralized, self-governing, network-based governance system would need highly integrated knowledge acquisition, storage, and AI-driven delivery systems of that knowledge to accelerate humanity's social and technological research and development. Huge governmental knowledge databases should not only be made available to shepherd governance systems because those databases are also part of the "press" that should be made available to all media consumers. Humanity's accumulated knowledge and future knowledge should always be made available to every sovereign individual.

The process of TMC is greatly enhanced when there is a free flow of information within a society that is delivered to individuals by media channels that minimize and expose the contamination of that information by sinister indoctrinating narratives, and the corruption of that information can be readily uncovered by media consumers through various means provided by a DSMN.

Chapter Four
Content Created by Artificial Intelligence (AI)

National and worldwide shepherd governance systems such as the United Nations continue to develop and implement policies about the usage of AI that reveal that they want to bring AI power under the centralized control of shepherd ruling elites within SSHs that have abusive centralized governance systems. According to one article published on July 18, 2023, the United Nations wants to govern AI as the following quote reveals.

"The United Nations (UN) should create a new international body to help govern the use of artificial intelligence as the technology increasingly reveals its potential risks and benefits, according to UN Secretary-General António Guterres.

The UN has an opportunity to set globally agreed-upon rules of the road for monitoring and regulating AI, Guterres said Tuesday at a first-ever meeting of the UN Security Council devoted to AI governance."[4]

What gives the UN or any shepherd governance system the right to be constantly "monitoring and regulating" anything a sovereign individual or independent business does anywhere at anytime with AI? Malevolent ruling elites within centralized governance systems around the world are feverishly working towards developing AI-driven governance systems that support tyrannical rule over vast human herds of exploited individuals. Humanity should have never been herded into a large number of vast human herds controlled by malevolent, shepherd ruling elites within a SSH thousands of years ago. The human race still has not learned how to live outside of a SSH. Humanity is a vast network of sovereign individuals that should live under a self-governing Network of Sovereign Individuals (NSI). AI-driven governance systems should have at the top of its governance hierarchy a self-governing NSI within each country created by individuals who follow the good side of human nature. AI-driven software, apps, and machinery that empowers individuals come from the good side of human nature. Lately, more and more AI-driven software and apps are made available to individuals that empower them to create different types of popular content, and such content created by AI should be free from the autocratic control of centralized, shepherd governance systems. AI-generated content is another form of "the freedom of speech." One type of AI-generated content is the creation of digital art from a text prompt that is created by a digital artist. The availability of digital art is now widespread across the Internet.

Below is an image created from the text prompt, "An Art Nouveau inspired landscape. The scene is lush and vibrant, with stylized trees and flowers. The colors are rich and saturated, with a focus on greens, blues, and yellows." Below is a black and white version of the full-color output generated on the NightCafe platform (creator.nightcafe.studio). See notes at the end of this book for the link to the full-color version.

img2

After entering the text prompt, the image above was generated in about one second. Because the creation of the above image requires the creation of a text prompt by a digital artist, the artwork itself should receive copyright protection. Also, digital artists usually do not accept the first AI generated output as the image above. Usually, a digital artist will greatly modify or enhance the above artwork using various tools that can add wildlife, people walking in the above landscape, or enhance the colors in the full-color version.

The simple image created by AI on the previous page is only one type of content that AI can create. AI can also create narratives for children's books, computer code, websites, news articles, and much more.

Here is a prompt to generate an explanation on how to create a JavaScript object from a JSON string. The explanation was generated by ChatGPT (chat.openai.com) Prompt - "How do you convert a JSON string into a JavaScript object?"

"To convert a JSON string into a JavaScript object, you can use the built-in JSON.parse() method. This method takes a JSON-formatted string as input and returns a corresponding JavaScript object. Here's how you can do it:

```
// Example JSON string
const jsonString = '{"name": "John", "age": 30, "city": "New York"}';

// Converting JSON string to JavaScript object
const jsonObject = JSON.parse(jsonString);
console.log(jsonObject);
```

In this example, **jsonString** is the JSON-formatted string, and **JSON.parse(jsonString)** converts it into a JavaScript object, which is then stored in the **jsonObject** variable. The **console.log(jsonObject)** statement will print the resulting JavaScript object to the console. Keep in mind that the JSON string must be properly formatted, with all property names and string values enclosed in double quotes. Otherwise, the **JSON.parse()** method will throw an error."

Everyday more AI-generated content is finding its way into the media world, and many centralized governance systems feel that they should apply special copyright laws to AI-generated content. The U.S. Copyright Office had the following on its website in 2023. "Today, the U.S. Copyright Office launches a new initiative to examine the copyright law and policy issues raised by artificial intelligence (AI), including the scope of copyright in works generated using AI tools and the use of copyrighted materials in AI training. This initiative is in direct response to the recent striking advances in generative AI technologies and their rapidly growing use by individuals and businesses."[5]

Protocols designed to filter AI-generated content to be included in a DSMN are needed. Does TMC mean that digital artists should reveal that their art was created with the help of AI tools? Should any content generated with AI tools require an explanation to the media consumer of how the media content was created?

Currently, artists who create a physical oil painting for sale do not need to provide a description of the physical tools used to make the oil painting. No artist needs to reveal to a potential buyer of his oil painting the types and sizes of the paint brushes he used, type of art canvas, the brand of his oil paints, or how he mixed the different colors of oil paints to get a unique color blend to use in his oil painting. A digital artist also should not have to reveal which AI tools, AI-generation platforms, or any digital apps he used to make his digital art. Anyone purchasing a piece of art would know if it was a physical oil painting or digital art, but requiring more governance regulation over digital art than an oil painting would be needless governance overreach.

Media consumers of image, video, or text content of a political or intellectual nature would also like to know if the AI used to generate such content was biased in any form. For example, many feel that ChatGPT is biased to the left-leaning side of the political spectrum. The process of making AI-created TMC may need special AI or SAI to monitor and analyze any AI-driven tools or platforms to determine if its generated output of content has any level of bias, and such bias should be described in a way that the average media consumer can understand.

AI created by individuals whose moral character leans towards the good side of human nature will always be an asset to the process of TMC. AI created by people whose moral character falls on the bad side of human nature should be put in its proper place where it can do the least amount of societal harm. The legacy media which includes print books and clay tablets in thousands of locations around the world cannot be modified or erased by malicious AI. The legacy media are protected from the malicious side of AI because they are not in the digital world. Print books and clay tablets include the copies of humanity's major world literature and other important print media going back thousands of years to the first literature in human history in Kiengir written on clay tablets. The first epic poem, the Epic of Gilgamesh, and the first children's lullaby in human history were written on Sumerian and Akkadian clay tablets using cuneiform.

Chapter Five

Why the Shepherd Ruling Elites Created the Indoctrinating Narratives

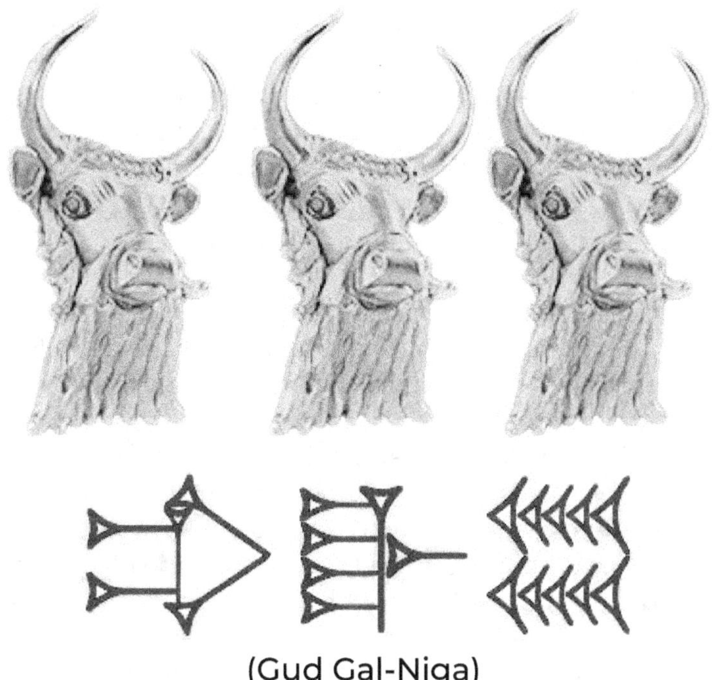

(Gud Gal-Niga)

Note: The Standard of Ur referred to in this chapter can be viewed in depth at the British Museum's website (britishmuseum.org).

The kings in Kiengir wore a shepherd hat crown showing their ties to the shepherd belief system of the first Sumerians who were nomadic pastoralists that settled in the Tigris-Euphrates valley where the Ubaidian people were living. With their flocks of sheep, goat herds, and cattle, the Sumerian ruling elites utilized many practical skills learned from their shepherd ancestors that enabled them to control large herds of different types of animals that they exploited for wool, beef, and more. The king wore royal kaunakes which were sheepskin skirts with the skin turned inside and the wool combed into decorative tufts. The kings of Kiengir always wore a shepherd hat crown to symbolize their role as shepherds of the brutally exploited Sumerians. The kings of the Akkadians who later conquered the Sumerians continued to wear a shepherd hat crown.

The predatory, shepherd ruling elites of Kiengir closely guarded their control of the propaganda narratives that were created in written and image forms. TMC that could have freed the minds of the people of Kiengir from living in social and psychological corrals as exploited human herds was almost non-existent. The shepherd ruling elites controlled the scribal schools and the scribes who wrote down the propaganda narratives on clay tablets. The shepherd oligarchy also controlled the artisans that created the statuary and the images that supported their indoctrinating narratives.

What were some of the reasons why the malevolent, shepherd ruling elites of Kiengir utilized indoctrinating propaganda narratives? To understand why the predatory, shepherd ruling elites of Kiengir resorted to mind control over the people in each Sumerian city state, we need to take a brief look at the time period before the Akkadian conquest and occupation of the Sumerian city states. The Sumerians were surrounded by Semitic peoples such as the Akkadians and Elamites. Being nomadic pastoralists in a time period when the Earth was sparsely populated, their language appears to have developed without much influence from other peoples, so it was a language isolate. After settling where the Ubaidian people were, they eventually turned Ubaidian towns such as Ur and Uruk into large Sumerian city states. Later, with the creation of large-scale agriculture, large low-wage human herds were necessary to work on the farms. All the Sumerian city states developed a SSH with a small shepherd ruling class at the top of the governance hierarchy. The tyrant class in each city state was like an organized crime family, and they were frequently at war with the other crime bosses of the other city states.

Images of Shepherd Ruling Elites

img 4 - Sixth Amorite Shepherd King Hammurabi (Louvre Museum) of the Old Babylonian Empire with a shepherd hat crown. The early Babylonians adopted much of the Sumerian beliefs and way of life. The head of Hammurabi shows Akkadian influence.

img 5 - Sumerian Shepherd King Gudea (2080–2060 BC or 2144-2124 BC) of the city state of Lagash with elaborate shepherd hat crown. His folded hands signify that he was a King-Priest of Lagash.

img 6 - Early Sumerian King-Priest (3300 BC) from the city state of Uruk wearing an early form of a shepherd hat crown and folded hands that signify his role as both a shepherd king (sipa lugal) and a priest - compare to img 5. On the banquet side of the Standard of Ur, one way to identify the priests is by looking at their hands. What was the exact nature of Sumerian political and religious indoctrinating propaganda narratives?

img5

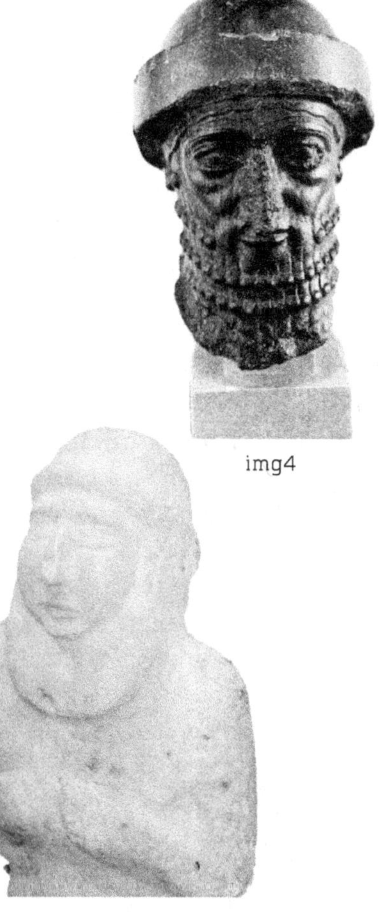

img4

Image 6 represents a time period when the predatory Sumerian shepherd kings were historically closer to the advanced, large-herd-control ideas of the nomadic Sumerian pastoralists. Image 6 is also one of the earliest known statues that symbolically show support for both political and religious indoctrination narratives.

img6

Needing armies to go to war with the other city state crime families for more territory, tribute from conquered city states, and gathering more human herds to exploit, the men and boys of Kiengir needed to be indoctrinated to willingly enter slaughterhouse battlefields where they could be mercilessly and painfully butchered as a herd of cattle. A Sumerian battle ax could inflict deadly, painful damage to any sovereign individual's body. Indoctrinating propaganda narratives were both religious and political. Initially, city-state wars were small-scale compared to the post-Akkadian, Sumerian Renaissance period when large-scale battles occured. The Standard of Ur now in the British Museum (britishmuseum.org) is image propaganda of a large-scale slaughterhouse battlefield.

Why was the battle depicted on the elaborate artwork of the Standard of Ur not a small-scale military skirmish? Each Sumerian and Akkadian city state army had its own type of military skirt distinguishable by the pattern cut at the bottom of each military skirt. The Standard of Ur shows four different military skirts from four different Sumerian city state armies and three different military skirts from three different Akkadian city state armies. A battlefield with seven different city state armies is not a small-scale military skirmish. The banquet side of the Standard of Ur depicting a victory celebration is also a large-scale banquet showing the Sumerian king and nobles celebrating their victory against the Akkadians. The Sumerian king is shown wearing the royal kanaukes and is shown as the largest person at the victory celebration which is an example of the proportional-size propaganda technique used in ancient Sumer, the propaganda of the Soviet Union, Nazi propaganda, and other time periods. If you look closely, you will see that the Sumerian king's head goes beyond the symbolic ceiling meaning he is above everyone else. Conquered Akkadians and Sumerian slaves are shown bringing animals to slaughter for the banquet and other things for the feast, and they are led by a priest which shows the importance of using religious indoctrination to strengthen the mind control over sovereign individuals. Behind the priest leading the servants is another priest holding a flute. In the top tier of the banquet side of the Standard of Ur, there is also a special priest signified by his long hair, and he is next to another man holding a harp. Sumerians and Akkadians were also fond of music which is a characteristic of basic human nature; however, the priest shown holding a flute suggests that religious music may have also played an important role in the religious mind control of both the Akkadians and Sumerians.

After the battle shown on the war side of the Standard of Ur, the conquering Sumerian king became the "King of Kings" of both Sumer and Akkad, so one reason for the victory banquet was to honor the Sumerian king's new status. There was no ceremony honoring the thousands of war dead. The Sumerian oligarchy utilized indoctrination to herd innocent men and boys into slaughterhouse battlefields, and they also utilized indoctrination to herd sovereign individuals into a lifetime of servitude as slaves.

The tomb of Queen Puabi gives us clues as to the nature of the enslavement of Sumerian sovereign individuals and how religious indoctrinating propaganda narratives helped keep the sheeple trapped in a social and psychological servant corral. Queen Puabi's royal tomb had more wealth buried with her than any other royal tomb found in Ur. Buried with Puabi were the bodies of fifty-two servants/slaves and a team of oxen harnessed to a ceremonial sledge. The dead slaves in the tomb were either poisoned or died of violent blunt force trauma. The large number of murdered royal slaves attest to the predatory nature of Sumer's organized religion that supported the idea of a make-believe Sumerian afterlife that needed murdered servants to serve royal elites in the Sumerian heaven. Reinforcing the idea of an imaginary, fictional afterlife by killing slaves to serve a dead shepherd ruling elite in some fake heaven was only one way to reinforce their religious propaganda.

Another reason why the shepherd ruling elites of Kiengir used indoctrinating propaganda narratives was to mentally herd sovereign individuals together as a slave-labor herd to fulfill the ruling elites' fanatical, narcissistic desire to construct large monuments and temples to symbolize their power and wealth. The Eanna Precinct in ancient Uruk contained temples and several buildings that housed the predatory ruling elites. It is estimated that the construction of the larger buildings in the Eanna Precinct would have required some 15,000 laborers to work ten hours a day for as long as five years to build all the buildings. The temple to Inanna was larger than the Parthenon in Athens. The Akkadians and Babylonians also worshipped Innana, but gave her the name Ishtar. Those at the top of the female social hierarchy were very powerful in Uruk and the other city states. The shepherd ruling elites of Uruk also imposed the first recorded predatory tax in human history on sovereign individuals which was the crop tax which was recorded using proto-cuneiform. The crop tax was another way for the shepherd ruling elites to claim sovereignty over the land and food.

There were many reasons why the predatory, shepherd ruling elites of Kiengir resorted to using sinister, indoctrinating propaganda narratives, and we have briefly described some of them in this chapter; however, the complexity and cunning craftiness of their deceitful societal narratives was a real, masterful work of art, and shepherd ruling elites today continue to use many of their mind-control methodologies. Shepherd ruling elites in Kiengir skillfully used collectivist, well crafted narratives that when woven together created detailed, complex, human-herd gathering ideologies such as Sumer's religious ideology that reinforced their questionable religion; however, as far as we know, they did not preach that nature itself was created by an entity outside of creation. In practice, it was a pagan religion, and its rulers constantly turned a blind eye to the innate religious needs of the Sumerians.

Did any of the sovereign individuals of Kiengir write anything against the tyranny of the malevolent shepherd ruling elites? Tablet #36 in the Library of Congress can be described as the first instance of political satire in human history written long before such literature was written in ancient Greece. The Sumerian writing shown on page 27 pronounced, "Gud Gal-Niga," refers to a "great fatted bull" which the scribe used as a coded satirical reference to a corrupt sipa lugal (shepherd king) or shepherd ruling elite who grows fat with wealth and power by exploiting others. The writing on tablet #36 satirizes Sumerian lords and kings in a time period when predatory shepherd ruling elites forced sovereign individuals to worship their rulers as living gods and goddesses. The narrative is written in a code-like manner since the brave scribe who wrote it would have probably been executed if his real message was uncovered. The scribe's play on words such as between the words lu-gal and lu-mah where lu-mah is written in a curious code-like manner in the context of the sentence to disguise the meaning of the story. In certain linguistic contexts, lu-mah and lu-gal can refer to the same thing. Think of a slight deviation in pronouncing a word in a purposeful higher or lower pitch in an utterance to change the meaning of a word as in a tonal language. Was there a group of rebellious scribes and other freedom-loving Sumerians communicating in this code-like manner? We do not know, but there are thousands of tablets that have not yet been deciphered. What will the clay tablets of Kiengir someday reveal? We do know that Sumer's centralized, shepherd government was totalitarian. Today, there are many "great fatted bulls" who do not want the truth about them to be widely revealed.

Throughout human history, malevolent shepherd ruling elites
have been responsible for the death and suffering of unknown
numbers of innocent men, women, and children. Humanity
continues to live under a SSH with a centralized governance system
in every country that exploits vast human herds of sovereign
individuals which continues to perpetuate the needless death and
suffering of innocent sovereign individuals. To weaken the political
power of predatory, "great fatted bulls," humanity should implement
decentralized governance networks and decentralized media
networks. The original Founding Fathers of the United States risked
their lives and wealth when they rebelled against an English
shepherd king, and the scribe who wrote the political satire on tablet
#36 also risked his life and wealth when he produced his code-like
writing on a clay tablet and that narrative is still not completely
understood, but it gives us a greater understanding of predatory,
shepherd ruling elites. A gud gal-niga designs malicious
indoctrinating narratives to justify his status within a SSH and tohelp
the shepherd ruling elite herd sovereign individuals into social and
psychological corrals where they can be easily exploited to fulfill the
great fatted bull's psychopathic and narcissistic fantasies of having
omnipotent power and wealth.

Chapter Six

Ideology As a Tool of Mind Control

Most Americans do not know the difference between socialism and a free market economy and do not even have an elementary understanding or simple definition of socialism.

Socialism is an socioeconomic system whose political ideology strives to bring the major productive forces of a society under the totalitarian control of a centralized shepherd government. Under the socialist system, creators and producers of products and services follow government mandates about the quantity and quality of goods to be produced. Consumer goods are rationed by authoritarian planning boards with government bureaucrats deciding who has access to the goods and services they desire. It is a sinister ideological system that can easily camouflage which malevolent, shepherd ruling elites are the actual rulers if such shepherd ruling elites want to remain anonymous. Socialism is a Marxist-based ideology, and its deceitful ideas have entered every institution of the United States of America.

A free market economy is very different than a socialist economic model. Here is a description of a free market economy by CFI. "A free market is a type of economic system that is controlled by the market forces of supply and demand, as opposed to one regulated by government controls. It is opposite on the spectrum to a command economy, where a central government agency plans the factors of production and use of resources and sets prices. In a free market, companies and resources are owned by private individuals or entities who are free to trade contracts with each other." [6]

For socialism to be successful in implementing its totalitarian rule, it needs a powerful, centralized shepherd governance system, and such a socialist system has always made it possible for a small group of malevolent, malevolent, shepherd rulers to gain enough power to impose their tyrannical rule on sovereign individuals. A DGN would be compatible with a free market economy, but would be at political odds with a socialist socioeconomic system. A DGN governance hierarchy coupled with a free market economy would produce a prosperous, orderly society of sovereign individuals where the production and distribution of products and services are viewed as a fundamental human right that should be free from governance overregulation and predatory taxation by a centralized shepherd governance system. It is a basic human right to be able to create, produce, and distribute products and services that will generate prosperity for sovereign individuals.

The problem in the USA is that the freedom-loving ideas of Americanism continue to be replaced by the collectivist, freedom-killing ideas of socialism. Socialist ideas such as class envy, neo-Marxist group identity politics, a progressive tax system, and smearing capitalism continue to be cunningly and maliciously spread by the current crop of shepherd media ruling elites in the CMO. In the indoctrination factories called public schools in the USA, children are slyly taught that the individual must always subjugate to the collective by obeying government agents. What has been happening in the USA since the founding of the "Communist Party USA" in 1919 is the steady spread of Marxist ideology in all of America's institutions. The malevolent, shepherd ruling elites who want a socialist governance system to help them gather vast human herds of exploitable human beings are attempting to overthrow Americanism. A socialist governance system makes it easier for a small group of malevolent-shepherd ruling elites to gain political power. One problem with Marxist governance systems such as socialism and communism is that their ruling elites frequently resort to the mass murder of innocent sovereign individuals.

img2

According to the Victims of Communism Memorial Foundation, communism has killed over 100 million people. On their website it states, "Victims of Communism Memorial Foundation is an educational, research, and human rights nonprofit devoted to commemorating the more than 100 million victims of communism around the world and to pursuing the freedom of those still living under totalitarian regimes."[7] The Memorial Foundation's website is a highly informative online resource that everyone who believes in the human rights of all sovereign individuals should visit.

Socialist ideology is just a mind control tool that malevolent, shepherd ruling elites use to brutally exploit what they view as human herds of enslaved people. Such predatory ruling elites will use any political, religious, or economic ideology as a tool that will best let them control the minds of sovereign individuals so that the shepherd ruling elites can fulfill their psychopathic fantasies of having omnipotent power. They do not believe in any ideology or religion. The ancient Sumerian predatory, shepherd ruling elites used the ideology of a pagan religion complete with non-existent goddesses and gods as the tool to help them rule over the brutally exploited Sumerian people. There is absolutely no real proof that Enki, Enlil, Ninhursag, or any other of the Sumerian goddesses and gods ever existed except in the minds of the mentally-abnormal Sumerian ruling elites. Sumerian shepherd ruling elites were so intensely narcissistic and psychopathic that many of them publicly declared themselves goddesses and gods.

Throughout human history, the malevolent-shepherd archetype has caused unspeakable human suffering. Humanity's constant heavy burden since prehistoric times has been the existence of shepherd ruling elites who are power-hungry, narcissistic psychopaths, and the best way to keep such demons on a leash is for mankind to do away with its centralized governance systems that empower the demons of the human race. Humanity urgently needs to implement decentralized governance systems, and create a decentralized media or DSMN of the people, by the people, and for the people where TMC will always set sovereign individuals free from the deceitful, artful indoctrinating propaganda narratives of predatory, shepherd ruling elites. From the Assyrian Ashurbanipal to the German Adolph Hitler, shepherd ruling elites throughout human history have caused unknown numbers of innocent deaths and unspeakable amounts of human suffering. It is time for Humanity to leave the herds and return sovereignty back to individuals.

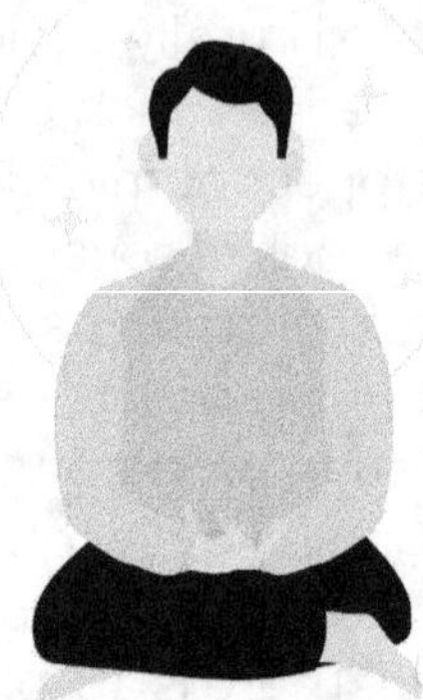

Chapter Seven

Human Herds or Sovereign Individuals

People are sovereign social beings who can voluntarily enter into social relationships guided by their natural biological nature. Children and adults develop positive social relationships among nuclear and extended family members, friendships with neighbors, and with others when they join a local sports team, a local church or synagogue, friendships with others in their workplace, and adult pair bonding. Individuals also develop social relationships with others as part of being a member of large groups such as a labor union or a national professional association for a specialty occupation. When are social interactions part of voluntary social relationships between sovereign individuals and when is manifest social behavior part of being a member of an exploited, groupthink-led human herd?

A sovereign individual can become part of an exploited, groupthink-led human herd when they lose some or all of their natural sovereign human rights, and those natural rights come under the control of predatory, shepherd ruling elites. Over 5,000 years ago, when the malevolent, "great fatted bulls" of Uruk imposed the crop tax on farmers, the Sumerians and the hardworking agriculturalists lost specific parts of their individual sovereignty. The crop tax gave the Gud Gal-Nigas sovereignty over the land, food, and beer. Beer was made using barley crops, and it was very popular among the Sumerians. The first known beer taverns in human history existed in Kiengir. A Sumerian queen who is also listed on the Sumerian King List is Queen Kubaba who started out as a beer tavern keeper. On the King list she is referred to as a lugal (king) not as an eresh (queen consort). The farmers of Kiengir grew barley, chickpeas, lentils, wheat, dates, onions, garlic, lettuce, leeks and mustard. A crop tax gave the "great fatted bulls" the sovereign power to control the ownership of land, and the price or value of food, and beer. The higher the crop tax, the higher the price of food and beer. After the crop tax was imposed, the land used to grow crops came under the sovereign power of the state. Essentially, the crop tax forcibly took sovereignty over land, food, and beer away from sovereign individuals and transferred that sovereign power over to the malevolent, centralized, totalitarian governance system in the Sumerian city state of Uruk that was ruled by the shepherd ruling elites. The agriculturalists became part of a human herd of farmers in Uruk after the crop tax was imposed on them because their sovereign rights over their own land and crops were forcibly taken away from them. Did predatory taxation become brutally oppressive in Kiengir?

Surviving inscriptions of Sumerian proverbs, sayings, and fables give us clues about the content of the daily thoughts of Sumerians, and they were written down on clay tablets by Sumerians and translated into English by ETCSL,[8] a project of Oxford University. Here is one that is TMC relating to predatory taxation which has been a favorite tool of tyranny used by shepherd ruling elites since prehistoric times. **"You can have a lord, you can have a king, but the man to fear is the tax collector!"**

How many Sumerians lived in "fear" of the tax collector? How much of the taxes collected went to support the lavish lifestyles of the malevolent tyrants or to finance their turf wars for power and wealth with other city states? The taxpayer human herd of Kiengir was brutally exploited.

Individuals can also become part of a malicious, groupthink-led human herd when their minds are possessed by a malevolent, venomous ideology. One such venomous ideology is extreme, radical feminist ideology. A venomous ideology acts like a venomous slithering serpent that purposefully sneaks silently into one's mind where it injects its toxicity into the natural thinking processes of its victims. Once poisoned, the victim's mind experiences psychological chaos that destroys their ability to follow the thinking processes of their own true inner self. They become possessed and controlled by the venomous ideas of the malevolent ideology. They start to behave as anyone who is demon possessed. The victim's thoughts are no longer their own. Here are a few real-world examples of venomous indoctrinating propaganda narratives listed on the wiki4men website. [9]

"I feel that 'man-hating' is an honorable and viable political act, that the oppressed have a right to class-hatred against the class that is oppressing them." Then Editor of Ms. Magazine - Robin Morgan

"The nuclear family must be destroyed... Whatever its ultimate meaning, the break-up of families now is an objectively revolutionary process." Linda Gordon

"I love the power women have. I think women rule the world because they rule men. Manipulating men - that's our job. That's what we're on the planet for." Isla Lang Fisher

"The more famous and powerful I get the more power I have to hurt men." Sharon Stone

Instead of promoting positive, enjoyable relationships between men and women, the venomous indoctrinating narratives listed on the previous page promote hatred towards men and boys, and they only serve to bring chaos to male-female relationships on both individual and societal levels. Robin Morgan's belief in "man-hating" is toxic, and such a belief arises from the evil side of human nature. Hatred itself is a malevolent emotion that only causes great psychological harm to hateful individuals themselves. A dynamic DSMN should always shine a very bright light on all venomous, human herd gathering ideologies so that TMC constantly reveals their true demonic nature.

A sovereign individual can become part of an exploited human herd when their natural sovereign rights are forcibly transferred to a group of predatory, shepherd ruling elites as in the case of predatory taxation. Sovereign individuals also become a member of an exploited human herd when they lose sovereign control over their own beliefs and natural thinking processes as in the case of venomous, malevolent ideologies, but an advanced civilization requires a more advanced social glue than our current, human-herds social hierarchy with its malevolent ideologies and lack of individual sovereignty. An important reason to create an advanced civilization is to increase the odds of the survival of the human race.

Sovereign individuals should come together in a way that cooperatively combines our individual creative power to invent and construct the technology that will increase our odds of surviving extinction-level events. Our sun will eventually die, and it is understandable why no one seems to care about that fact because that event is a few billion years away. In the final stages of hydrogen fusion, our sun will swell and become bloated. It will then consume Mercury and Venus for sure. If the sun's enlarging atmosphere does reach our world, Earth will dissolve in less than a day.

We know that we are living on a planet that will eventually be a dead planet or even dissolve meaning that it will one day cease to exist, but for unknown reasons, we continue to ignore the fact that other types of extinction-level events could happen at any time in the future. Extinction-level events not only could originate from outer space, but right here on Earth. Here is a brief quote from an opinion article by Scientific American. "Habitat degradation, low genetic variation and declining fertility are setting Homo sapiens up for collapse."[10] The title of this article is "Humans Are Doomed to Go Extinct."

Population decline from sub-replacement fertility, an asteroid impact, large-scale volcanism, a wartime nuclear holocaust, and other things could also start us on our journey to extinction. By some estimates, over ninety-nine percent of the total number of species that have ever existed on Earth have already gone extinct. The odds for the continued existence of the humankind are overwhelmingly against us.

There are also a great number of serious science and social technological skills that we do not have as a species that would greatly increase the odds of humanity's long-term survival if we had them. We do not know how to find habitable exoplanets for mankind to populate, and even if we found some habitable exoplanets, we do not know how to get to those habitable locations. We do not know how to stops wars and war crimes. Do we really know how to prevent a full-scale nuclear war?

We do not know how to stop the worldwide crime rates including child abuse, sex trafficking, carjackings, home invasions, murder, rape of men, women, and children, pedophilia, genocide, democide, and many other crimes. We do not know how to effectively control malicious, corrupt politicians and other shepherd ruling elites. We have not learned how to effectively control the bad or evil side of human nature.

Humanity has produced great scientists, philosophers, theologians, social thinkers, law enforcement systems, technology, and more, but it all has not been enough to design and create an advanced civilization that will propel humanity to populate our galaxy. We do not even have an operational "Civilization Science." Sumerians learned how to project their thinking into the future to plan for the next planting season or over several years when building the Eanna Precinct, but humanity needs to learn to project its thinking much farther into the future to avoid extinction.

If there is anything that unites humanity, it should be the shared goal of creating an advanced human civilization that will provide the societal hierarchical structure that accelerates the development of our civilization's social and science technology to the level where we can become a multi-planet species as soon as possible. Can humanity beat the odds so that mankind's journey becomes "Mankind's Eternal Journey?"

Civilization 2.0, 3.0, and Beyond Series

Book I: Civilization Version 2.0
Humanity's Future or Humanity's Extinction

Book II: Empowering Parents in our Failing Schools

Book III: The Art of Tyranny I
Introduction to Truthful Media Content

Info on all of our publications at: gebsmedia.com

gebsmedia.com

Notes

1 Team, WebX. "The 6 Companies That Own (Almost) All Media." Web FX, www.webfx.com/blog/internet/the-6-companies-that-own-almost-all-media-infographic/. Accessed 20 Jul. 2023.

2 Hub, Bible . "John 8:32." Bible Hub, 20 Jan. 2022, biblehub.com/john/8-32.htm. Accessed 20 Jul. 2023.

3 SAFE Network. "Secure Access For Everyone." SAFE Network, 16 Mar. 2020, safenetwork.org/. Accessed 20 Jul. 2023.

4 https://www.cnn.com/2023/07/18/tech/un-ai-agency/index.html Fung, Brian. "UN Secretary General Embraces Calls for a New UN Agency on AI in the Face of 'Potentially Catastrophic and Existential Risks'." CNN, 18 Jul. 2023, www.cnn.com/2023/07/18/tech/un-ai-agency/index.html. Accessed 20 Jul. 2023.

5 US Copyright Office. "Copyright Office Launches New Artificial Intelligence Initiative." US Copyright Office, 16 Mar. 2023, copyright.gov/newsnet/2023/1004.html. Accessed 20 Jul. 2023.

6 CFI Team. "Free Market." Corporate Finance Institute, 3 Apr. 2023, corporatefinanceinstitute.com/resources/economics/free-market/. Accessed 24 Jul. 2023.

7 Memorial Foundation. "Communism Killed Over 100 Million." Victims of Communism Memorial Foundation, 24 Jul. 2023, victimsofcommunism.org/. Accessed 24 Jul. 2023.

8 "The Electronic Text Corpus of Sumerian Literature (ETCSL)." ETCSL, 1 Jan. 2006, etcsl.orinst.ox.ac.uk/. Accessed 28 Jul. 2023.

9 "Feminist Quotes." Wiki4Men, wiki4men.com/wiki/Feminist_quotes. Accessed 29 Jul. 2023.

10 Gee, Henry. "Humans Are Doomed to Go Extinct." Scientific American, 30 Nov. 2021, www.scientificamerican.com/article/humans-are-doomed-to-go-extinct/. Accessed 29 Jul. 2023.

Img 1, img 2 - view color versions at: https://www.gebsmedia.com/artoftyranny/

img 3 - Image 3 was created by the author, Cornel Chavez, MA

img 4 - "Hammurabi, Louvre Museum" by lreed76 is licensed under CC BY-SA 2.0. To view a copy of this license, visit https://creativecommons.org/licenses/by-sa/2.0/?ref=openverse.

img 5 - ArchaiOptix, CC BY-SA 4.0 <https://creativecommons.org/licenses/by-sa/4.0>, via Wikimedia Commons

img 6 - ALFGRN, CC BY-SA 2.0 <https://creativecommons.org/licenses/by-sa/2.0>, via Wikimedia Commons

www.ingramcontent.com/pod-product-compliance
Lightning Source LLC
Chambersburg PA
CBHW070223260726
48658CB00006BA/2140